VISION TO RESULTS

Vision to Results

LEADERSHIP IN ACTION

Jim Fischetti

COPYRIGHT © 2019 JIM FISCHETTI

All rights reserved.

VISION TO RESULTS

Leadership in Action

ISBN 978-1-5445-1396-6 *Paperback*

978-1-5445-1395-9 *Ebook*

First, I dedicate this book to Jill—my best friend, partner, and mother of our children. Without her, I never would have achieved the success I have in life or business. Thank you!

Second, to my children Katie and Tommy, son-in-law Adrian, grandson Alastair, and granddaughters Fiona and Catherine. They are why I work as hard as I do.

Third, this book is dedicated to you, the reader. Those who strive to make a difference as a leader are truly the difference makers.

Contents

Acknowledgments

This book would not be complete without Ted Flanagan. The hours and hours we spent to create this were so rewarding. Thank you for your hard work and dedication to the process.

There are several people I'd like to thank for their investment in me. Without their wisdom, support, mentorship, and love, I'd not be the man or leader I am today:

Earl Fincher, an incredible leader, and an even better man.

Brenda Benson, you saw something in me and have always been a coach and cheerleader for me.

Mo Anderson, a true icon of business, you poured into me when you didn't have to. I've learned so much from you.

Gary Keller, being in your mastermind group transformed my mind and perspective.

Mark Cress, thank you for first putting the idea of a book into my head.

Mike McCarthy, you gave me the opportunity of a lifetime and the freedom to execute, while also challenging me to think bigger and deeper.

Sam Chalfont, the first person outside my family who knew I was going to succeed. His belief changed my life.

Michelle McBride, thank you for pushing me into speaking and teaching.

Paula Hoeft, thanks for showing me how to blend leadership and humility.

Jay Crow, a true gentleman and leader, your wisdom over the years has been invaluable.

Anthony Braswell, a great leader and pastor, who has been an example of love and kindness as he leads.

Bill Garrett, who left this world too young but filled his years with investing in people.

To the hundreds of authors who have poured into me through their books.

To my father-in-law, even though you're gone now, your words and wisdom still live on in my heart and mind.

To my dad, you were my first and last hero.

Introduction

The biggest vision in the room always wins. This might not be a new idea, but it's one that too many leaders forget. When leaders forget about the importance of vision, they are not the only ones who suffer—so does each member of the organization they lead.

In his book *The Innovation Secrets of Steve Jobs*, author Carmine Gallo examines vision as the core principle underlying the most fundamental societal change since Gutenberg. Gallo relates the story of a young software programmer named Rob Campbell. Nearly three decades before *disruption* became a buzzword, Campbell began to grow increasingly fascinated by the possibilities of personal computing. Campbell could sense in this emerging field a world-changing technology, and he wanted in.

At the time, there were only three players in the PC market: Tandy, Commodore, and Apple. Only one of these companies had a leader whose vision allowed them to understand that they were standing on the front lines of a revolution; the other two knew only that there was a little bit of money to be made.

Campbell went on a quest to claim his own place in the PC revolution. First, he interviewed with Tandy, the first giant in the world of personal computing. During the interview, Campbell asked a simple question: "What is your vision for the personal computer?" The response was less than inspiring. "We think it can be a huge hit in the upcoming holiday season," they told him.

Unsatisfied, Campbell next interviewed with Commodore. At the time, Gallo notes, Commodore's stock price hovered around $1 per share. Their response to Campbell's vision question? "We think the PC can help us get our stock price over $2 per share."

Utterly deflated by the myopia of these industry leaders, Campbell scheduled a lunch interview with Jobs, then in his first stint as CEO at Apple. Although Gallo doesn't say, it's not hard to imagine Campbell approaching this meeting with a certain amount of fatalism. Although Tandy and Commodore executives had each expressed to Campbell some sort of vision for their companies, he didn't feel compelled to join either. He didn't connect with their vision for their companies. The scope of what these companies wanted, and what they thought the PC could achieve, was far smaller than what the young and ambitious Campbell himself had for the technology. None of us would blame him for approaching the Jobs interview prepared for yet another disappointment. This was, after all, before Steve Jobs was *Steve Jobs*. At the time, Campbell likely thought of him as just another tech CEO with similarly shortsighted aims for the PC.

Of course, with the benefit of hindsight, we know that Steve Jobs was anything *but* just another tech CEO with limited vision and insight. Campbell learned this early on in the time he spent with Jobs on that day in 1977.

Campbell broke out his usual question early in their interview. "What is your vision for the personal computer?" he asked once again. This time, instead of a glib reply about holiday sales or vague promises for a boost in stock prices, Campbell's query was met with an impassioned response about the way the PC was going to change the way we work, how we actually *did* work, how we interact with each other, and how we educate our children and entertain ourselves. It took Jobs an hour to answer Campbell's question. Jobs explained his vision for the PC as one of the biggest advances in humanity since the development of Gutenberg's printing press.

Forty years later, I'd say Jobs was pretty spot-on, and not just about the future of the PC. What Campbell's experience reveals is the way a leader's vision can be both limiting and liberating. The fact that Tandy and Commodore are no longer with us suggests that it's not enough simply to hold a vision for your organization. True leadership involves creating a vision, communicating it with evangelistic fervor, and holding people accountable.

Simple enough, right? So why does it seem so rare in practice?

THE TESLA CONUNDRUM AND THE UBER FIX

Even products that ought to do well in a red-hot market might not perform well in the presence of shaky leadership. Consider Tesla, the electric automobile manufacturer. Consumers love Tesla. The demand for their products couldn't be higher. There's a waiting list to buy a car for crying out loud, and yet the company continues to struggle financially.

It has endured slowdowns in production. Layoffs. Staff turnover. Missed goals, particularly production numbers on their incredibly anticipated Tesla Model 3. At the moment, its very future seems less than assured.

Why?

The reality is that Elon Musk seems unhinged right now. He's all over the place. His Board of Directors basically had to order him to stop using Twitter. Being a visionary doesn't automatically make you a leader.

Musk is a great example of a brilliant guy who's not cutting it as a leader. He's performed poorly on investor calls and tried to intimidate people who had legitimate questions about the way Tesla is run. Ultimately, the biggest problem Tesla faces is a lack of clear expectations from the top. People don't know what Tesla is trying to accomplish. Want proof? I bet you can't answer this simple question: Are they a battery company or a car company right now?

Almost every one of the telltale signs of poor leadership is present in Tesla at the moment.

Now let's take a look at Uber. Once upon a time, not that long ago, Uber was in similar straits as Tesla. Travis Kalanick was a deeply flawed CEO. His poor people skills permeated the entire culture of the company, all the way down to the drivers. Morale was in the dumps. For Uber to find its way back to form, for it to fix its culture and begin hitting its performance targets, Kalanick had to go. The fix for Uber was a top-down deal that began with exchanging a leader who was unable or unwilling to execute a vision for someone who could.

It's a simple lesson but one fundamental to the message of this book: leadership without vision isn't leadership. A vision not communicated by the leader is merely "words on the wall." Holding your people accountable to live the company's vision is hard sometimes, but the opposite of love isn't hate. It's apathy. Accountability is an act of love.

ALL ROADS LEAD *FROM* A COMPELLING VISION

If you've recognized your organization in any of what you've read so far, great! I'm here to offer a solution. We'll delve into the mechanics of this solution as the book goes along, but it's important to understand off the bat that good leadership begins with a compelling vision.

That compelling vision is the answer to the big question. It's here that every leader must begin: What is this company about, and how are we going to achieve our goals?

We'll spend a lot of time talking about how to conjure up this compelling vision and, even more importantly, how to have the biggest vision in any room. For now, remember this: the most important thing you can do to make your vision a reality is to talk about it.

A lot.

In fact, talk about your vision until you can't talk about it any longer. Then talk about it some more.

Jack Welch, perhaps the single most-admired CEO in the history of modern American corporations, once said that he spent 70 percent of his working days communicating his vision to his employees. Upon retiring, he said his only regret was that he hadn't spent even more time at it.

When a leader gives this much care and attention to communicating their vision, a synergy between the troops and the leader will emerge, which manifests through the vision. If connection is one of the keys of corporeal success for any organization, then the consistent communication of a compelling vision is the muscle for that body.

MY VISION

As part of my four decades as a successful leader and executive, I've made it my life's pursuit to study leadership in all its forms. Over those years of study, I've come to a few conclusions that, once put into action, have proven incredibly effective.

I've used the principles I'll share in this book to grow a $4 billion organization of four thousand employees into one double that size and with $13 billion in revenue. I've had to figure out how to effectively lead nearly ten thousand employees spread across fifty different locations. I've enjoyed an incredibly successful and rewarding career building and leading corporations based on the principles of vision, communication, and accountability we'll be examining in depth throughout this book.

This book is the distillation of decades of thought, experience, stinging failure and immense success, and everything in between. In the pages that follow, I'll share with you all the principles that have driven my success and show you how they can contribute to yours as well.

Think back to Rob Campbell and the question he asked the execs at Tandy, Commodore, and Apple: *What is your vision?* If you were to ask me for my vision of what real leadership looks like and how to put that vision to use for yourself in ways that will improve your life both professionally and personally, this book would be my answer. It is my hope that you walk away with a perspective you haven't yet considered, a renewed energy to lead and get results for you, your people, and your organization.

As is probably clear by now, vision is the foundation of everything that will follow, and as you'll see, there is a crisis in leadership that begins with vision. Let's start there.

CHAPTER ONE

The Crisis in Leadership

We live in a time of corrupted leadership. Not *corrupt*, necessarily, but corrupted, for sure. Leaders who aren't accountable. Systems designed to protect the status quo at all costs. These are symptoms of a larger disease, and they are existential threats to the success and longevity of any organization.

The common thread running throughout this crisis is vision. As this book will show, organizations need a leader with a compelling vision, dedicated to spending lots of time—Jack Welch, perhaps the most famous CEO in American corporate history, would say almost *all* of their time—communicating that vision to their people and then holding everyone, including themselves and every member of the organization below them, accountable to carry out the goals identified in the vision. When these criteria aren't met, trouble follows.

Examples abound.

Wells Fargo, not that long ago, turned on their customers in the service of the almighty dollar. The leadership at Fox News created a toxic environment that was unhealthy for the people who worked there. Both the Roman Catholic Church and nondenominational megachurches such as Willow Creek saw instances where the institutions themselves initially sought to protect entrenched leaders and organizational power while failing to tackle immense moral failings of those same leaders.

Politicians on both sides of the aisle are all too eager to avoid tough decisions. Their vision has been corrupted from one of service to the greater good to one that has as its highest calling self-interest and preservation of power. In their quest to retain power and influence, doing anything is dangerous, and one hallmark of the corrupted leader is that they avoid danger at all costs. Gridlock and stasis are the inevitable result.

Most of us are familiar with the fight-or-flight response to change, challenges, or fear. There are really three:

- Fight
- Flight
- *Freeze*

Too many so-called leaders live in the "freeze" state.

That is one of the curious things about a leader who hasn't successfully conjured and shared the biggest vision in the room: it isn't always the actions leaders take but the things they are unwilling to do that causes the majority of the problems we see today.

THE COURAGE TO ACT

Like most Americans, I was transfixed by the destruction that visited Baltimore in April 2015. It was a fraught time in what has become an extended period of social turmoil. While in the custody of the city police department, Freddie Gray was severely injured while traveling in a police van to the station. He later died of his injuries. Occurring just months after nationwide unrest following the events in Ferguson, Missouri, among other racially charged incidents between police and minority civilians, it led to massive protests that escalated into days of rioting and destruction.

As I observed the evolving disaster, one thing I noticed was the equivocation of city and state political leaders.

BALTIMORE RIOTS OF 2015

- April 12, 2015—resident Freddie Gray is arrested by Baltimore police
- During his transport inside police van, Gray is injured and lapses into a coma
- Gray died April 19
- Even before his death, large protests developed, escalating into full-blown riots, eventually requiring deployment of the Maryland National Guard
- State of Emergency not lifted until May 6
- The resulting riots resulted in:
    - 486 arrests
    - 113 injured police officers
    - At least 2 shootings and 1 woman critically burned in associated arson
    - 350 businesses damaged and/or looted (including 27 drugstores)
    - 150 burned cars
    - 60 building fires
    - More than 1,000 police officers and 2,500 National Guardsmen needed to restore order

I have spent almost four decades devoted to the study of leadership, and what I saw transpiring in Baltimore shocked and dismayed me. In a situation that demanded firm and immediate action, everyone wavered. Inaction bred inaction and ultimately led to the escalation of the Freddie Gray protests from lawful exercise of civil disobedience into near anarchy.

I felt that a clear solution was at hand if only a leader in Baltimore had the courage to see it. But everything I saw suggested that city and state leaders were improvising, making things up as they went along. There was no evidence of a unifying vision apparent in any of the leadership's response to the riots. In that vacuum, violence escalated.

After the second day of rioting, I had had enough.

"Honey, I'd end these riots in five minutes," I proclaimed to Jill, my lovely wife, who has patiently listened to my various pronouncements over three decades of marriage.

She looked at me with that certain sideways glance she has and said, "What would you do, Jimmy?"

"First thing I'd do, if I were the governor, I'd call the Baltimore mayor and tell her I've got a press conference scheduled five minutes from now and that that conference is going to go one of two ways. One, I'll tell everyone that she's requested assistance from the National Guard and that I'll be sending them to restore order. Or two, I'll tell everyone she *hasn't* asked for National Guard help, but I'm sending them anyway."

Regardless, I would have had the courage to act because, like any good leader, I knew the situation demanded action. In fairness, the Freddie Gray riots came at a difficult time in contemporary American history, which certainly played a role in the failure of political leadership to exercise any. The riots in Ferguson, Missouri, were still fresh in the public mind, and political leaders walked a dangerous tightrope.

My empathy is limited, though. A leader without a vision is not a leader, and worse, a leader with a vision who does not take the time to communicate that vision incessantly is a leader without portfolio. Their vision is just words on a wall without the moral authority behind them to put vision into action.

This is especially true in a world like ours, where leaders are afraid to fail forward. Perfection is an unattainable ideal. Failure itself is underappreciated. Failure can be a gift because it is in that failure that a growth occurs. We idolize the image of the infallible leader, unfortunately, someone who can do no wrong.

Nothing worth achieving simply arrives as a fully formed, successful apparition. In current conditions, though, failure—or to be more precise, the *fear* of failure—leads to paralysis. Leaders who worry about failing are leaders inclined to do nothing in the first place, and that's clearly what I observed going on in Baltimore.

INSTANT GRATIFICATION

The need for instantaneous results has only exacerbated the problem. Bandwidth is difficult to find, with leaders today unable to make space for themselves to think and plan and enact their vision. With social media and wall-to-wall media coverage, there's also no *anonymity to act* these days. Leaders no longer have the room to figure things out, so deficiencies in vision inevitably lead to colossal, public failures of the kind that don't easily lend themselves to correction. The moment a statement is made or an opinion shared or a decision even hinted at, thousands or even millions of people instantly have the ability to question and second-guess.

Don't confuse this idea with a call for less transparency. Open covenants openly arrived at, to paraphrase one of Woodrow Wilson's Fourteen Points, are still the best way to operate, but there also needs to be space to be wrong or to adjust decisions that don't work out as planned. Perfection is nearly impossible to attain in the real world; but when a leader doesn't have the space to be wrong, far from ensuring that only the best decisions are put into action, this insistence on a standard of perfection only ensures that leaders take the most cautious route possible—and greatness rarely results from meekness.

Thankfully, the idea of creating space for failure is gaining traction in some areas of business. The Securities and Exchange Commission, for example, is rumored to be considering a fundamental change in its reporting requirements for publicly traded companies. Currently, those corporations need to submit financial reports quarterly or every three months. The frequent pace of financial reporting forces companies to operate on extremely short timelines that don't allow for experimentation. Worse, if a change in business practices does not result in immediate success, often companies won't wait to see if time is the cure and jettison potentially good ideas early in their gestation.

The rumored change would reduce reporting requirements to twice a year, thus allowing corporations more time between reporting deadlines, time that organizations could use to decide whether business decisions are working or need tweaks. Longer time spans between required reporting would allow space to think and breathe, and give time for good ideas to take root.

THE MOB BELIEVES IN ACCOUNTABILITY. SHOULDN'T YOU?

Vision is a precarious thing. A leader can create a compelling, wonderful vision, execute its communication like a pro, and share with the people they lead deep connection through the vision. However, if there are no mechanisms for holding both the leader and the led accountable for achieving the mission or, worse, if the leader lacked real commitment to the vision in the first place, there can be real consequences. The Mafia knows this. That is why the cost of accountability can be dire. Even in noncriminal enterprises, the price for failure to hold people accountable to the vision can be steep.

A TRAGIC COST

Accountability is a safeguard against failure, and as we will discuss in later chapters, it is an act of supreme care. Leaders who hold their charges accountable to the vision are, in fact, expressing a kind of love for their people. The crisis in leadership today occurs because too many leaders lack the intestinal fortitude to hold people accountable, and it shows in every arena of public interaction. It can even have deadly consequences.

Consider the tragic case of University of Maryland football player Jordan McNair.

In spring 2018, Jordan was a promising offensive lineman getting ready for his first season of big-time college football. During a practice on May 29, 2018, McNair cramped up during a series of sprints before becoming increasingly weak. His condition worsened enough that, about forty minutes after the initial symptoms of heat injury showed, McNair was carted off the field and back to the trainer's room. A half hour later, McNair's mental status changed, he suffered a seizure, and he was taken away by ambulance.

Doctors treating him in the emergency department discovered his body temperature had reached 107 degrees. His condition deteriorated, and he was transferred to the intensive care unit, where things did not improve. McNair, nineteen, never recovered, and died on June 13, the result of heatstroke.

The ensuing investigation revealed a troubled culture in the Maryland football program. Players reported punishing practices and a culture of playing through pain, not itself abnormal in the sport but to a near-inhumane degree. The report issued by the independent sports medicine consultant reviewing the incident was scathing, noting that it took ninety minutes from the time McNair first became ill until an ambulance was finally summoned, by which time the series of physiological destruction that took Jordan's life was already underway.

Media reports—like that in the *Washington Post*, for example, which called Maryland football an "abusive culture" that "might have contributed to the player's death"—did not help.*

Clearly, university leaders had not held the program's coaching staff accountable to the stated vision of intercollegiate athletics to which they supposedly subscribed. Worse, accountability for what happened on that Maryland football field in May 2018 was a long time coming. Initially, the team's head trainer and the assistant athletic director in charge of training were each placed on administrative leave. The team's strength and conditioning coach also resigned.

Head Coach D. J. Durkin, the program's leader and the architect of its culture, was initially placed on administrative leave as he sought to keep his job, even while his team played the 2018 campaign without him. In a particularly tone-deaf move, the University Board of Regents voted to reinstate Durkin on October 30, 2018.

The backlash was instantaneous and fierce and included players walking out of a team meeting with Durkin. The lack of accountability permanently disconnected Durkin's vision for the team from the group of young men

* "U-Md. Releases Report on Jordan McNair, Laying Out Timeline that Led to Player's Death," *Washington Post*, September 21, 2018.

he counted on to achieve it. The coach's actions alienated him from the people who counted on him most. The next day, Halloween, university president Wallace Loh fired Durkin.

TOO LITTLE, TOO LATE, AND PROBABLY FOR THE WRONG REASON

Loh did the right thing twice in this instance, and yet it was probably too little, too late. First, he apologized in August to the McNair family about two months after Jordan's death. Then, on Halloween, he undid the regents' misstep of reinstating a coach who had failed in his main duty in almost every way and fired Durkin.

His apology was particularly compelling, as we don't hear statements like that in the halls of power every day. The hard truth, though, is that his statement didn't come for nearly two months and largely not until national media outlets such as ESPN reported on McNair's death and the controversy surrounding his treatment as a football player at Maryland. The vision that bound the Maryland football program together was violated the day Jordan McNair left football practice for the last time in an ambulance. They can rebuild that trust with a new vision and new leaders who will hold themselves as accountable to the vision as they hold their players, but it will take time.

In situations where accountability is missing, you often see leaders failing to act until outside pressure of some sort is applied. The default position is inertia because it is easier and feels safer to do nothing.

While observers may give credit to Loh and the university for holding Durkin accountable, I'd suggest that it's not true accountability if it's forced on you. Leaders are accountable because their moral code assures them it's the right path to take and because they know that their organizations can't exist in a culture where no one is held to task for their actions—or inaction.

This may seem an extreme example of what can happen in the absence of a compelling vision, but I share it to give you an idea of how seriously I view the subject.

THE MOB GETS IT

Real leadership requires a certain kind of strength, which is to say the strength to do the right thing, not the thing that necessarily feels the best. Leadership is not for the weak of mind or character. As an extreme example of this, consider the Mob. Forgetting for the moment the moral peril of their profession, as an organization, they understand that real leadership requires a strong vision, a bias toward action, and a commitment to accountability. Their vision of leadership is "family first," and they are committed to it.

While translation as a principle to the corporate or nonprofit world is inexact, the thing to understand is that in their way, the Mob has a total commitment to accountability and vision. They deal immediately and ruthlessly with those in the organization who don't adhere to the leader's vision, and their dedication to accountability—if not their methods—is second to none.

They are so committed to the overall vision that they are not afraid to off somebody if the situation requires it. Obviously, this isn't in alignment with the values of humanity in general, but there's a useful lesson here.

Consider this: the Mob is actually "removing" a poor performer from the organization and isn't afraid to fire someone. Most of us could be more committed to removing bad performers, negative actors, and even mediocre people from our organization quicker. Much quicker.

The reality is that there are immoral organizations out there doing a much better job insisting on strong leadership, and thus getting results, than some "moral" organizations.

THE LEADER NEEDS TO "GET IT" BEFORE ANYONE CAN JOIN THEM

One of the great gifts a leader with a strong vision gives

their people is an understanding of where their work fits into the mission of the organization. Much has been made lately of the idea of connecting work and social worth, with one noted London economist going so far as to write an entire book on the notion of "bullshit jobs," jobs for which the lack of meaning in work clouds the making of money with a patina of near shame. (See David Graeber's *Bullshit Jobs: A Theory* for more.) I have quarrels with some of Graeber's points, but the thesis of his idea has the ring of truth: jobs that don't require a strong vision from leadership are almost always hard, if not impossible, to connect with emotionally, and work without worth is hardly worth doing.

To extend the Mob metaphor a bit, the strength of the vision its leaders hold informs the average hit man's decision to never attack civilians not involved in the trade. Civilians are a necessary part of their ecosystem, the ones who bring much of the money into the criminal economy.

Another example is the hospital janitor. In an organization where the leaders have communicated their vision of good health to all areas of the organization, the janitor understands the importance his or her work has to the larger vision and mission. The janitor working for a leader who communicates their vision and holds people accountable to it understands that how well they do their job actually saves lives.

INSPECT, DON'T EXPECT

The sad reality is that few corporations are genuinely in alignment with their own vision. This misalignment leads to larger troubles, and unless a leader is actually inspecting the work being done by the people under them, there is no incentive for that person to course-correct.

The US Marine Corps has a saying: inspect, don't expect. Simply put, it's not enough for a leader to have a vision. They also have to have the courage and dedication to ensure that the people below them are living out that vision.

Ultimately, it starts with leaders who are willing to hold themselves accountable to their own vision, and then inspect and ensure that they're holding the people below them accountable.

THE FIRST STEP: FINDING YOUR VISION

One thing I hope I've made clear so far in this examination of the crisis of leadership in America today is that the first step in becoming the leader you want to be is to find and articulate a vision, both for you and for your organization. In the next chapter, we'll examine the fundamental importance of vision as the biggest single thing a leader brings to the table.

Great organizations, such Nordstrom, are guided by great visions. In the next chapter, we'll examine what an effective vision looks like in practice and how you can find one too.

CHAPTER TWO

It All Begins with Vision

Early in my career, I traveled the country as a trainer for a real estate organization. I often traveled far from home on business, and the job demanded a professional appearance at all times. I had recurrent nightmares centered on the possibility that an airline would misplace my luggage. Eventually, the nightmare manifested, and on a trip from Raleigh to Tampa, where I was scheduled for a major presentation, I arrived at the airport, but my suitcase did not. The airline had misplaced my luggage.

I took stock of the situation: I was stranded in Tampa, luggageless, at night, and with mere hours before my big talk. Things were dire.

Panicked, my first stop was a men's clothing store in the local mall. This was before the days of "suit separates," so anything I bought would need tailoring. The men's store had a jacket that fit, but the pants needed hemming, and it was too late in the day for that.

Sensing my desperation, the salesman offered a suggestion. "There's a Nordstrom on the other side of the mall. They may be able to help."

At the Nordstrom, I made my case to their salesman. I had a black coat waiting for me back at another store, but I still needed a pair of properly hemmed black pants. The Nordstrom salesman looked confused.

"Wouldn't you prefer an entire suit, where the coat and the pants match?" he asked.

"Absolutely," I answered, "but it's got to be too late in the day to get everything tailored tonight, and I need this for a meeting first thing in the morning."

The salesman said he had an idea.

"Our tailor left for the day a little while ago, but if I could get him back in here, and if he could alter and have a suit ready for you tonight, would that be a better solution for you?"

I initially attempted to talk him out of calling his tailor. It never occurred to me that the tailor would ever return to the store to work on one suit.

But I really needed that suit.

A little lost for words, I nodded assent with vigor. I was convinced they wouldn't be able to accommodate me, but I was in no position to turn down any offer of help.

"Give me a couple of minutes, and let me see if I can reach my tailor," he said. Five minutes later, he said he had good news, that he had been able to reach the tailor and that he was on his way back to the store to work on my suit.

Twenty minutes later, I was fitted and eating dinner in a nearby restaurant while the Nordstrom tailor worked his magic. Within a couple of hours, I was checked into my hotel with a brand-new, custom-tailored Nordstrom suit in my hands.

To this day it remains the most money I've ever spent on a suit, and one of the most satisfying purchases I've ever made.

A COMPELLING EXPERIENCE

Anyone familiar with Nordstrom's vision for customer

service would be unsurprised by this story. The chain's commitment to customer service is legendary. Its stated mission is to provide customers with the most compelling shopping experience possible, and they are notorious for the lengths they will go to live up to that vision. My Tampa suit emergency was ample evidence that this vision was alive and well at Nordstrom.

The salesman and the tailor in this one particular Nordstrom store understood the vision of their leaders intrinsically and fully. Remember, I tried to talk the salesman out of calling his tailor. My understanding of their vision was limited to what I thought was possible. The thing I thought to be impossible—buying and tailoring a suit on such short notice and so late in the day—they understood to simply be part of the Nordstrom vision.

Nordstrom leaders had taken the time to craft a vision for the company, an act that a surprising number of organizations don't. More importantly, they communicated that vision to the people who worked for them to the point where everyone in their chain knew the vision and could explain it as well as their leadership.

Nordstrom is based in Seattle, yet in a store more than 3,100 miles away, the hourly employees understood what Nordstrom's vision and mission was. I am certain that I would have had a similar experience in any Nordstrom in the country, given what a thorough and successful job the company's leadership had done in communicating its vision.

Can someone walk into any location in your organization and ask, "What's the vision of this organization?" What answers, if any, would they get? Could they share how that shows up in day-to-day activities?

The recipe for how a good vision penetrates to the heart of what a good company does is simple: the leader establishes a vision, communicates that vision frequently, connects with their people through that vision, and then holds them accountable. The recipe fails, though, without its most important ingredient: the vision itself.

PITFALLS

While external forces can bring difficulties into the process of establishing a vision, the most common problems often arise from within. Leaders fall prey to several common pitfalls when it comes to creating a coherent vision for the entire organization.

FAILING TO SPREAD THE WORD

Jack Welch, the former CEO of General Electric and undeniably one of the most revered leaders in American corporate history, was once asked how much time he spent communicating his vision for the company. He estimated he'd spent 70 percent of his time over the years communicating the vision, and his only regret? That he hadn't spent more.

A vision that is not communicated (subject of the next chapter) isn't a vision at all. Leaders who keep their visions for their organizations in their heads are essentially blind.

It's the simplest of ideas, and yet like many simple ideas, it was among the most important lessons I learned as I developed as a leader. Too often, leaders think there's got to be more to it, that there has to be a grander scope to this earth-shattering activity of being the head honcho.

They don't understand one key idea: success is simple; it's just not easy.

EXCLUSIVITY AND COMPLEXITY

An insecure leader often needs reassurance that no one else could do the job but them. Emblematic of this need is the unstated hope that others in the organization will observe the work of the leader and say to themselves, "There's no way I could do that." In this case, the complexity is a way of cementing the leader's importance to the organization but at a cost. Organizations that depend on complexity will never achieve the full scope of its leader's vision.

For this type of leader, the main symptom is a need to make things much more complicated than necessary. The leader creates a role for themselves that is nearly impossible for anyone other than them to perform. Due to this exclusivity and complexity, even a well-communicated vision is going to be difficult for members of the organization to adopt and support. They are both baffled by and excluded from the leader's vision.

NORDSTROM BY THE NUMBERS

- Founded in 1901 in Seattle
- 380 stores in 40 states, Puerto Rico, and Canada
- About $15 billion in annual revenue
- Approximately 72,500 employees
- Ranked 72 on *Fortune* magazine's Best Companies to Work For, and is a Hall of Fame member of the same list
- Also owns:
    - HauteLook
    - Nordstrom Rack
    - Trunk Club

LACK OF EXECUTION

Vision is meant to stir activities to get results. Don't make the mistake of thinking that vision alone will do it. You have to work at measuring activities and results to ensure that you get the results you want: the vision becoming a reality.

Bryan Stolle, in his blog post "Vision without Execution Is Just Hallucination," rightly warns that we need to roll our sleeves up and get after it.

No vision is a big problem—so is no execution.

THE VISION OF SAM WALTON AND WALMART, TECH DISRUPTORS

We've seen how important the leader's vision is for any organization. There's nothing *more* important. How the leader arrives at their vision is as idiosyncratic as the leaders themselves.

There are some tried-and-true steps to creating your vision:

1. Start with your goal or purpose. Be clear about what you want to see happen.
2. Put time into perspective. How far in the future are you looking? Ensure you go far enough out that you

get past the present-day situations/concerns/challenges.

3. Reflect on prior successes. Remember the positive accomplishments you, your team, or your organization have accomplished. Celebrate them. This offers a chance for a positive and expectant mindset and a powerful vision.
4. Write it without any limiting beliefs. This is simply a first draft. Be fearless.
5. Review and revise the first draft, the second, the third, etc. Continue until you've got it.
6. Get feedback from trusted advisors. Revise if necessary.
7. Finalize it.

Now, you're ready to share it.

One of the dictionary definitions of *vision* is a mental image of what the future will be or could be. Let's start there. As a leader, your main purpose is to create a mental image for your staff of what the future will be or could be. This is Jack Welch's first edict of what a great business leader does. They create a vision. That's job one for any leader.

There is no industry immune to this need. Sam Walton, founder of Walmart, one of the world's largest corporations, was recently described in a magazine article as the country's first tech CEO. Those familiar with the folksy biography of the Arkansas entrepreneur might have difficulty thinking of Walton in that way, but there are some compelling parallels, and they stem directly from Walton's vision for what retail could be.

When he opened his first store in Rogers, Arkansas, in 1962, Walton's whole vision was indeed focused on changing the way retail was done. He wanted to revolutionize the department store model and make it more cost-conscious, thus allowing him to sell at cheaper price points. To that end, Walmart innovated across the spectrum of its operations. Sam's stores were among the first retailers to computerize delivery, supply systems, and sales processes.

This resulted in a huge savings in operations costs, which allowed the vision for cost-containment, and outpricing its competitors, to become reality. Sam Walton's vision began with the ability to see a better way to run a retail operation and then disrupting the status quo by putting that better way into practice.

IT'S NOT JUST FOR WALMART EITHER

While conjuring the vision for your organization might lead you to innovation a la Sam Walton's notions for Walmart, sometimes all it requires is for the leader to reimagine processes that already exist.

WALMART BY THE NUMBERS

- Founded in 1962 by Sam Walton in Rogers, Arkansas
- Headquarters in Bentonville, Arkansas
- Nearly 12,000 stores nationwide
- Revenue in 2018 of $500 billion
- 2.3 million worldwide employees, 1.5 million in the United States
- Such a force that studies show a Walmart built in a new market decreases its competitors' sales by 40 percent

Casper and Purple are two companies bringing huge change to the way mattresses are bought and sold. The technology of the mattresses themselves isn't much different than the traditional box-spring-and-mattress arrangement. The difference arises from the idea of doing away with the traditional furniture showroom approach to mattress sales, choosing instead to sell directly to the consumer online and then deliver the pieces directly to your home.

Casper and Purple—and their imitators—are making great products, but that isn't the real genius behind their appeal. Their leaders clearly began with a vision for a better mattress and, more importantly, a better way to sell them. Other industries are beginning to poach their ideas as well, as we've seen in everything from selling cars (e.g., Carvana) to selling mortgages (e.g., Rocket Mortgage from Quicken Loans).

Carvana, for example, allows consumers to purchase their next vehicle completely online and then have that purchase delivered to them or, even more unusual, picked up at one of the company's "car vending machines." Every step of buying a car, minus perhaps the test drive, can be completed online, entirely negating the need for a dealership. The middleman is disappearing, and without him, prices will also drop.

What we are witnessing with the arrival of these three companies are organizations in which the leadership first had a vision for a new way of doing business. Only time will tell whether those visions will succeed, but each represents a reimagining of entire segments of traditional business operations, and that journey doesn't begin without leadership possessing a vivid idea of the potential futures for their companies. It all begins with the vision.

SCOTT BORAS AND PAYING THE PROFESSIONAL ATHLETE

We see this idea of a compelling vision in places other than retail. Take a look at the sports entertainment industry. Scott Boras remains one of the best players in the history of the University of the Pacific baseball program, where he was a prolific hitter. After college, he toiled in the minor leagues for four years before knee problems forced him from the game. Neither of these things are why his name is likely familiar to you, even if you are not a fan of the game.

Were the college and minor league baseball careers the most important aspect of Boras's baseball résumé, he'd likely be nothing more than a footnote in the game's long history. But in the early 1980s, Boras felt called to work on behalf of baseball players, whose earning potential had traditionally been unfairly limited by the game's owners. He formed the Boras Corporation and dedicated himself to his vision of raising the salary of baseball players.

Boras's vision turned out to be compelling enough that in 2014, *Forbes* magazine ranked the Boras Corporation as the most valuable single-sport agency in the world. His impact on sports is hard to overestimate. His name alone attached to a player is enough for some teams to decide not to pursue a particular athlete. He's so successful that some teams avoid signing his players rather than face a negotiation with him.

One startling example of Boras's clout and almost Svengali nature is the case of Tom Hicks, who bought the Texas Rangers from George W. Bush in 1998. Two years later, Hicks signed a Boras player, Alex Rodriguez, to a multiyear, $252-million contract.

BORAS CORPORATION BY THE NUMBERS

- A baseball-only sports agency
- Named Most Valuable Single-Sport Agency in the world by *Forbes* in 2014
- Regularly sets records in contract values for its clients
    - First $50 million contract (Greg Maddux, 1997)
    - First $100 million contract (Kevin Brown, 1998)
    - First $200 million contract (Alex Rodriguez, 2000)
- Headquartered in a $20-million, 23,000-square-foot building in Newport Beach, California
- Subsidiaries:
    - Boras Marketing (memorabilia, marketing, endorsements)
    - Boras Sports Training Institute (conditioning, sports psychology)

The interesting thing to note is that Hicks bought the *entire* team for $250 million. Boras is so good at what he does that he convinced Tom Hicks to pay $2 million more for A-Rod in 2000 than he paid for the entire team just twenty-four months earlier. Scott Boras had a compelling vision about how professional athletes should be compensated, and his ideas altered the salaries for an entire sport.

He did it by taking a stand for the players. Even though free agency existed at the time, allowing players more freedom of choice as to where they played and how much they earned, there was also lots of collusion between the owners to keep salaries relatively low, at least in the early days.

In addition to pay, Boras and his company attend to his clients' other needs. They provide access to nutritionists, doctors, even financial advisors. As part of the vision for complete customer service, they take care of their players in ways other agencies typically do not, all of which stems from Boras's vision for what athlete representation should look like. Zig Ziglar is famous for this idea that if you help enough people get what they want, you'll get everything you want.

THE COMPELLING EXPERIENCE BEGINS WITH A COMPELLING VISION

Boras understands that if you do what you're supposed to do—in his case, take care of the players whose futures rest in his hands—the rest will take care of itself. Success is almost inevitable if the leader first begins with crafting a compelling vision for their organization.

Steve Jobs didn't set out to become a billionaire or to boost the stock price of his fledgling company or to spark brisk holiday sales. He was determined to revolutionize the personal computer and, in the process, bring it to the wider world. His vision was compelling, and from that compelling vision arose one of the most important companies in American (or anywhere, for that matter) history.

It's rare for the person with nothing but financial motives to achieve massive success. Making money is great, but it's hardly the basis for a compelling vision on which to base the hopes of an entire organization.

Nordstrom, Apple, the Boras Corporation, GE under Jack Welch—these all have at their core and within their DNA the compelling visions of their leaders.

WORDS ON A WALL

As we'll see in later chapters, a vision that is not communicated to the people on your team—and one that isn't protected, supported, and acted upon—is no vision at all. It's merely words on a wall. College football provided a striking example of this in summer 2018.

The Ohio State football program and head coach Urban Meyer came under fire when it was revealed that an assistant coach Meyer had hired had been accused of domestic violence on more than one occasion in recent years. Questions immediately arose as to what Meyer knew and when about the assistant coach's spousal abuse, which dated back to at least 2009.

Meyer fired the assistant as soon as news of the accusations appeared in the media, but Ohio State eventually suspended Meyer for three games in the 2018 season. Meyer would retire after the season-ending Rose Bowl.

Meyer's complicity was abhorrent on many fronts, not the least of which was the way it violated the football program's vision of respect for women. Meyer may not have committed the actual abuse, but his failure to uphold the vision of the program meant that that vision was nothing more than trite words painted on a wall.

THE GREAT NORDSTROM TIRE REFUND

Compelling visions lead to compelling outcomes. I lived a personal example of the Nordstrom commitment to customer experience when they sold me my last-minute suit. It remains the most I've ever spent on a suit, and I would do it again happily.

Another such outcome is possibly apocryphal in origin, but regardless, that the tale continues to be told, that it rings so absolutely *true* to the mission of the venerable department store, speaks volumes for the extreme lengths Nordstrom goes to in order to keep its customers happy and live the vision its leaders had for offering the best possible experience.

In most versions, the story goes something like this:

Alaska, 1975: a customer returns to the store where they bought a set of tires. Although the physical building once housed a tire or auto parts store, it was now a Nordstrom. In the story, the dissatisfied customer wheeled their set of tires into the clothing store—which has never sold tires in its history—and was promptly issued a refund. On a set of tires Nordstrom had never sold.

The moral of the story is that Nordstrom knew that by refunding this small amount of money (relative to the overall operations of the chain), they'd have a customer for life. It was a simple decision, especially if you're committed to your vision of offering a compelling customer experience.

COMMUNICATION MAKES THE VISION REAL

Jack Welch, former CEO of GE, made clear what he saw as the most important part of his job: communication. As a leader, he spent three-quarters of his day communicating his vision up and down the ranks at GE. When asked after retirement what he'd have done differently, he said he would have spent more time communicating.

In the next chapter, we'll examine the ways a leader ensures everyone in the organization understands and knows completely the vision that underpins everything they do.

CHAPTER THREE

Great Visions, Communicated

We remember the great Martin Luther King Jr. for the amazing vision of racial equality and justice he enumerated in some of the most famous orations and writings in American history. Less remembered are the lengths to which King went to spread that message.

King only lived to the young age of thirty-nine, yet he managed to ingrain himself permanently into world consciousness through the simple technique of communicating his vision with religious fervor and dedication. The intensity of his work ensured that his vision was communicated far and wide, and his vision has defied even the passing of time.

It is estimated that in the eleven years he was active, King traveled at least six million miles and spoke twenty-five hundred times, reiterating over and over his message of social justice and peaceful protest. He was a great communicator, and this simple act of communication forever changed the country.

By the time he died, I doubt there was an American alive who didn't know what King was all about. It is easy to overlook the shear enormity of his communicative efforts in today's age, where a 280-character Tweet can reach hundreds of millions of people in an instant. During the years of King's mission, the internet did not yet exist. The mass media was clumsy and disjointed, and yet King was able to reach millions upon millions of people with his vision. This is because he was clear, concise, consistent, and constantly communicating.

CLARITY

Leaders have to achieve absolute clarity in delivering their vision. Muddled thinking at this stage of the process will lead to inevitable confusion among your people. Clear articulation while creating the vision is critical to ultimately achieving it. King's clarity lent his vision the credibility it needed, especially in a 1960s America not predisposed to see or hear it in the first place.

The dictionary defines *clarity* as "the quality or state of being clear." The verb *clarify* is a good reminder to leaders. It means to make understandable or to free from confusion. Those are pretty good marching orders.

CONCISION

A compelling vision does not mean one that takes inordinate amounts of time to communicate. The human attention span is at an all-time low and not getting any longer. Time is limited to communicate your vision, so being concise has rewards beyond simply taking less time. Clarity may be the difference between your people aligning with your mission and their discarding it as more white noise in the midst of a day overflowing with it.

Mark Twain famously said, "I didn't have time to write a short letter, so I wrote a long one instead." It takes more time and effort to be concise, but it is worth it. Being concise will push aside the unnecessary. A big advantage of having a "tight" vision is that people won't get sidetracked with things that are actually outside the goal.

Do not confuse *short* and *concise*. "Be nice" is short, yet it can cover many issues and is not necessarily as concise as your vision.

CONSISTENCY

King's message never changed, no matter the audience. He was consistent in the face of incredible travails—no matter whether he was being punched, shot at, or in the end, sacrificing his own life. No matter what came his way, he never wavered. The recent Nike campaign featuring controversial former NFL player Colin Kaepernick included the tag line, "Believe in something. Even if it means sacrificing everything." The clarity of King's message resonates almost fifty years later in this sneaker and athletic clothing ad.

Remember that consistency is also about being in alignment with what you say. Is what you are saying a match for how you operate? Gandi's words are a strong reminder of this: "I'd be a Christian if it were not for the Christians."

CONSTANTLY COMMUNICATING

Think about those stats from earlier in the chapter:

- Six million miles traveled
- Twenty-five hundred speeches
- Eleven years

Add to that how many sermons King delivered, books he wrote, papers he published. It's easy to praise him for being prolific, but that prolificacy is nothing compared to the passion for a vision that underlaid it all. He spent nearly every working hour constantly communicating his vision.

Many leaders make the mistake of thinking that communicating a vision is a one-and-done scenario. They too often think creating the vision, then communicating it once is sufficient. King knew intuitively what I'm saying expressly: communicating the vision requires constant attention.

Be sure to communicate via multiple methods:

1. Stories
2. Elevator pitches
3. Social media
4. Videos
5. One-on-one sessions
6. Inside the organization
7. Outside the organization

THE GREATEST COMMUNICATOR

Whenever I'm asked to name the best communicator I've witnessed in my lifetime, one person stands out from the rest: President Ronald Reagan.

Reagan was first elected in 1980. That was almost four

decades ago, and yet most people of voting age at the time can tell you what he believed in. The list was concise and clear. Reagan believed in limited government, defeating Communism, and the idea of America as a light to the rest of the world. How do I know that? Ronald Reagan communicated his vision relentlessly, combining his natural charisma and speaking ability with a concise, clear message.

Most impressive of his achievements was his ability to connect his vision genuinely with the people. His vision was not designed to be bait on a hook. The message was not crafted by a focus group designed to feel its way around to what would resonate with the public. The things Reagan espoused were his heartfelt beliefs, and he was relentless when it came to sharing them.

IF YOU TRY TO ACCOMPLISH EVERYTHING, YOU'LL ACCOMPLISH NOTHING

The peril of the Cold War can't be overstated. Two sides, mired in enmity, armed to the teeth with nuclear weapons trained on each other—the stakes were existential. Any hair-trigger excuse could have ended the world.

That peril increased when the initial model of "appease and coexist," in place since the end of World War II, failed to make the world any safer. Reagan understood that the

Russian government of the time wanted to vanquish the United States as much then as fundamental Islam and ISIS does now. He knew that the only path to true safety lay in the West winning the Cold War.

Not everyone agreed. The intelligentsia and those in professional government believed we could coexist. Reagan was in the minority. Through his constant communication with the American people, his idea of defeating Communism and his belief in the spirit of Americanism and pulling ourselves up by the bootstraps took hold. During Reagan's two terms in office, we witnessed the fall of Communism, unprecedented economic vitality at home, and an era still remembered as one of the most successful in national history.

And it all began with one person with an incredible ability to communicate his vision.

HOW TO KNOW IF YOU'RE BEING HEARD

Many years ago, I was the leader of a firm in Oklahoma City. My vision for the organization was that we treat each other like a family. I communicated that mission clearly and often. We valued taking care of each other.

One of the first times that vision was tested, I passed the communication test with flying colors. A tornado had torn through the nearby city of Moore, Oklahoma. The twister destroyed the home of an employee's relative. Putting my vision of care for each other into action, we went to work raising money and doing whatever we could to help the family of our employee. Within five months, we'd rebuilt that home, the first to be erected in the entire city following the storm.

I did not get to bask in the glow of that success for long, and I had no one to blame for that but myself. A few months after we finished rebuilding that house, I got a call no father wants to receive. Middle of the night, and my daughter phoned to say that her house was on fire. It was a terrifying time. Thankfully, no one was hurt in the fire, but the house was going to be uninhabitable for quite a while.

I'm a private person by nature, and I did not immediately share with my people what had happened. I didn't see a reason. Unlike the tornado house, my daughter's was fully insured. She and her family were safe, the house would be rebuilt with insurance money, so I counted my blessings and kept my troubles to myself. Of course, what I did not, or could not, see was that this attitude was in violation of the vision I'd spent so much time communicating to my organization, that we were a family that cares for one another.

One day not long after, two of my leaders came into my

office and closed the door. They looked serious. Hurt. Angry even.

"You fraud," one began. "You say we're a family, you have this major need, and you don't tell us?"

She was genuinely hurt and mad.

She was also 100 percent correct.

Through my inaction, I'd violated the vision I'd spent so much time communicating to them. Worse, my privacy devalued the vision itself. Despite any chagrin I may have felt, part of me was pleased. A major component of my vision for the organization was accountability, and these two leaders had held me accountable. They were not afraid to speak truth to power.

That afternoon, I sat down and emailed the entire organization, filling them in on my daughter's situation. Meanwhile, the two women who'd chastised me got to work and raised $13,000 overnight and sent it by FedEx to my daughter and her family.

That's commitment to the vision, which let me see clearly that I'd done a good job communicating it to them. All the proof I needed was there. We weren't paying lip service to our vision. Our vision had become who we were.

My daughter's experience differed. At the time of the fire, she worked for a nonprofit that served people. This was an organization whose founding principle was care and concern for other people, and yet that's not the reaction she got when her bosses learned of the disaster that had befallen her.

The fire took place on a Friday night. Over the weekend, she phoned one of her bosses to tell them about the fire. Her boss had two things to say in reaction.

"I'm sorry to hear that. I'm still going to need you to come in on Monday."

Unfortunately, what my daughter experienced is typical for so many parts of the working world. The irony was not lost on me. My daughter worked for a nonprofit with the stated aim of helping people, yet in her moment of need, they had no help to offer her. Meanwhile, I worked for a for-profit company that went out of its way to care for people, including my daughter, who was not an employee.

Much like the Ohio State situation, if your actions don't support the articulated vision and mission, then that vision is just a bunch of words on a wall.

COMMUNICATING THE VISION REQUIRES SPEAKING IT AND LIVING IT

The best vision in the world left uncommunicated is no vision at all. It's an idea, a potential vision, but without sharing it, a vision lives in isolation, and a vision kept in isolation is self-defeating. There is one easy way to know if you've done a poor job communicating your vision: no one should ever tell you that your vision is the organization's "best kept secret."

This last point is the secret sauce to all of this discussion about communication. If the leader who creates the vision isn't also motivated to do the things necessary to accomplish it, if the leader doesn't buy into the vision, how can they expect that from anyone else? The answer is clear: they really can't expect anyone to pick up the slack, or to take the vision and run. Many books have been written about leadership, but they rarely examine the leader's responsibility to not simply communicate the vision but to live it too.

Leaders are in the odd position that they have many conversations in their heads that no one else hears. The vision is a burning desire of theirs. They're thinking about it constantly and imagining ways to implement it. The trap is that it's easy to fool yourself into believing that because the vision is the preoccupation of your thinking life from dawn to dusk, then you've communicated it to your people too.

The classic example of this is the good ol' boy who's been married for decades. One day his wife says, "I wish you'd tell me you love me more often."

"Darlin'," he replies, "I told you once. If I change my mind, I'll let you know."

Most leaders approach communication this way, but the reality is that this method of communication is doomed in a relationship and in getting a leader's vision to permeate the organization.

ENGINE OF CHANGE AND CONNECTION

Communicating a vision is a great engine for change, whether it's within your organization or in the world at large.

Martin Luther King Jr. is a powerful example. Less than five decades after his murder, which itself was only a few years removed from the Jim Crow South, the country elected its first black president. In addition, King left behind a legacy of social justice movements whose work continues today.

In the next chapter, we'll examine what happens when you put these two pieces together: the compelling vision communicated without cease.

The whole is always stronger than its component parts, and a compelling vision communicated zealously leads to a connection between the leader and the led that is strong enough to change an organization or even a country.

CHAPTER FOUR

Connecting the Dots

I'm a devoted football fan. I love watching the NFL. Any fan who's paid attention to the game for the last seventeen years has witnessed the amazing success of the New England Patriots.

Theories abound regarding their dominance, ranging from superior coaching and playing to a bendable interpretation of the rules. The answer is neither complex nor arcane. The franchise has reached unprecedented heights of success because it has leaders with a compelling vision to win championships who then communicate that vision with discipline and vigor, and the players respond.

Between owner Robert Kraft, Coach Bill Belichick, and the face of the franchise, eventual Hall of Famer Tom Brady, at the helm, the three leaders of the team connected in a shared vision of success. By ensuring that they surrounded themselves with players and coaches who shared that vision, who *connected* to the leaders through it, the Patriots have become one of the most successful teams in this or any other sport.

NO OVERNIGHT SUCCESS

The Patriots success was not assured. Before the arrival of Belichick and Brady, Robert Kraft owned the team through some lean years. It took him several attempts to purchase the team of which he had been a season ticket holder since the early 1970s. In 1994, he finally took control and led the team to some decent results—including the 1996 Super Bowl the team lost to the Packers—but also to a streak of mediocrity.

Kraft had a vision to bring a championship to New England, and Coach Bill Belichick believed he knew how to get it done. Before the Patriots, though, little in Belichick's background suggested he would one day ascend to the throne as perhaps the best coach in the game's history. He'd had success as an assistant to Bill Parcells on the Giants' staff that won a Super Bowl in 1986, where he was known mainly as a defensive specialist, and one decent season as head coach in Cleveland in the early 1990s.

Tom Brady was an unheralded sixth-round pick in the

2000 NFL Draft who didn't even start on his college team in Michigan. In a league where every physical attribute is measured and quantified, the traits that made Brady one of the best of all time eluded the experts.

Sometimes, though, the most important things aren't easily observed. For the Patriots, the mix of imperfect elements came together in a perfect way, and it began with a vision connecting three men dedicated to a shared vision.

WHY IT WORKED IN NEW ENGLAND AND COULD FOR YOU TOO

For those unaware of the results, these three men combined to create the most successful franchise in modern sports history. As of this writing, they are still on an unprecedented run of Division Championships (eleven) and consecutive appearances in the AFC Championship Game (seven), and have won five Super Bowls since 2001.

This amazing run is the direct result of players connecting to the leadership through a compelling vision. Kraft, Belichick, and Brady have consistently communicated to everyone around them the vision they have for bringing championship football to New England year in and year out. While the cast of characters around them changes annually, the compelling vision combined with constant communication means that no matter who's on the team from year to year, the players and leaders connect through that vision.

In terms of a corporate structure, Kraft, Belichick, and Brady are C-Suite executives. Kraft operates like a chairman of the board, Belichick is the CEO, while Brady is the chief operating officer in charge of executing the vision on the field. All three are key leaders, but the reality is that the vision started with Kraft. Ultimately, it was Kraft's commitment to winning championships that lured Belichick away from the New York Jets, the team he was set to take over as head coach. Imagine how that franchise might be different today save for that one development!

The Patriot Way, as the methodology behind the franchise's success has become known, works because everyone stays connected through the championship vision. There were many ways that this could have collapsed. After his early success, if Tom Brady had decided he needed to be the highest-paid quarterback in the league, that would have taken a leg out from the championship vision. There wouldn't have been enough money available to spend on the supporting players who added the ingredients necessary for the team to win.

COMPELLING VISIONS REQUIRE ALIGNMENT

The ever-present danger, though, is that visions become

misaligned. Priorities change, and the focus gets blurry, and once the leaders and the led are no longer aligned, things can get tricky.

The Patriot Way has worked because the three men at the top of the organization have remained in a kind of symbiosis for years. However, beginning in the 2017 season, observers noticed cracks in the facade. Belichick and Brady seemed to no longer be on the same page, and pontificators heralded the end of the dynasty.

Of course, the Patriots promptly won another AFC Championship and a trip to the Super Bowl. As the 2018 season dawned, doubts remained about whether Brady and his coach were indeed still connecting through a shared championship vision. As of this writing, the jury remains out on that count.

What is not in doubt is that in order to continue connecting through the shared, compelling vision, the leader and his or her people need to be aligned, need to share a vision for what can be achieved, and need to show how to go about achieving the vision.

Any organization facing these challenges will have a host of questions to answer. For the Patriots, there are several. Does Belichick want to prove he can win without Brady? Does Brady now want to prove that the team's success had more to do with his on-field excellence and not Belichick's planning?

FLATTENING THE HIERARCHY

When everyone in an organization connects through a shared vision, one of the interesting results is that these connections tend to flatten hierarchies. The worth of each person is directly related to the fact that each of them plays a necessary role in executing the vision.

In a culture in which every member of an organization is equally important to achieving its mission, leaders can afford a vibrant sharing of ideas and healthy discussions. Equality begins with connection, and in an organization where the leaders and their people are connected through the vision, there are no competing interests on the agenda. This connection heads off any competition between possible visions. The group has decided on its communal focus and can work toward reaching goalposts rather than worrying about which goalposts are out there in the first place.

IT'S ABOUT MORE THAN COUNTING HEADS

Leaders at the luxury Ritz-Carlton hotel chain ensure their people remain connected to the chain's vision for the "wow" customer experience through weekly Friday huddles. Staff members are encouraged to give examples of ways they've provided amazing experiences to their guests. The hotel is committed enough to its vision of customer service that they allow staffers to spend up to $2,000, no questions asked, to take care of customer needs.

These huddles put a human face on the metric of success. If all the leadership did was count vacancy rates in the hotel or measure only the profit margin, if they weren't engaging their staff often to gauge their alignment with the company vision, they'd miss out on the most important data of all.

Anyone can count heads. The secret to ensuring the staff is connected to the vision is to create measurables, which in this case are the stories staffers relate about customer engagements that live out the Ritz-Carlton vision.

Creativity is a key component of this process. It is no small matter to get people to tell stories showing how they're carrying out the vision without being prosaic and just outright leading them to the question you really want answered. These stories can be beautiful, and no leader worth his or her weight is going to tire of hearing stories about their vision being executed.

RITZ-CARLTON BY THE NUMBERS

- Corporate ancestry dates back to 1911; current structure established in 1983
- 130 luxury hotels worldwide
- Headquartered in Chevy Chase, Maryland
- Approximately $3 billion in annual revenue
- 40,000 employees
- The Ritz-Carlton Gold Standards are taught across a variety of industries
- The Ritz Carlton Shanghai was voted by Condé Nast readers as the best hotel in Asia

DELEGATING FUN

Having fun is an underrated metric to ensure that staff is connecting to the vision. Not every leader comes equipped to be the jovial type, though. Leaders can benefit from a trick I learned, which is to designate a fun captain.

How do you know if you need to name one of these? Walk around your office. Are people cutting up? Is the sound of laughter absent from your halls? Offices in which people aren't having fun are also most likely offices that aren't hitting their goals.

In my organizations, I'll often name a fun captain and

give them a single charge: make sure people are having fun here. People willing to laugh and have fun are people who feel safe where they work, and who likely feel connected to their leaders through the shared vision for the company. The leader creates—or does not create—this environment where people feel safe and valued.

ARGUMENTS CAN BE PRODUCTIVE TOO

The worst thing in life is to live in fear. Fear is also the sign of a dysfunctional organization. Creative tension is an amazing force for progress and innovation, but workers who live in fear of disagreeing with the leadership will keep all their best ideas to themselves. Worse, they might decide against pushing back against the leader's mistakes.

Disagreements mean employees feel safe. When my two colleagues closed my office door and led off the conversation with the words "You fraud," they knew my vision of family and transparency allowed them to be honest like that with me.

Leaders create that atmosphere. When people are afraid to have vibrant, even heated, discussions, it means they don't feel safe or heard. They don't feel secure. While being collegial is a good thing, leaders need to ensure that they've created an atmosphere that has room for disagreement too.

THE BEST IDEAS COME FROM YOUR PEOPLE

One of the biggest benefits of connecting with your people through the vision is that it brings out their best work. Great leaders know to harness this principle to get the most from their workers. If your vision includes space within it for your people to expand their skills, explore their interests, and bring their best ideas to the office, so to speak, you will maximize the chances of success.

Google's famous "20 percent rule" is an amazing example of this in action. Regardless of their role at the internet giant, Googlers (as their workers are affectionately known) are encouraged to spend 20 percent of their work hours tinkering with personal projects. This effort has produced some of Google's most important contributions.

If you've ever used Gmail, then you've experienced the fruits of this indulgence. Gmail stemmed from one Googler's desire to create a better email system. It was part of one particular Googler's 20 percent allocation, not their actual job at the company. The best leaders include in their vision room for connections they never anticipated.

This policy also resulted in Google's AdSense program, which enabled a deeper level of monetizing information to promote ad sales. By using algorithms to target ad revenue, AdSense has increased both Google's business and the business of their customers.

As effective as this 20 percent project was, Google actually ended it five years ago. The project is alive and well, though, in numerous companies such as Apple, LinkedIn, and Microsoft. Although their programs are slightly different, they all provide space and time for employees to work on projects that they are passionate about but that exist outside their duties. This is a great business strategy because it creates new products and fulfills their peoples' desire. Studies show that millennials, in particular, hold as a core value the ability to work on side projects while at their regular job.

This is a great example of the workers connecting with leaders' vision to create an amazing tool such as Gmail and many of the Google products that have arisen since. Google's vision included creativity and innovation, and their people have responded.

BIGGEST CONNECTION OF THEM ALL

It bears repeating that communication of the vision never stops, *especially* once you've connected with your people through that vision. Communication is not a one-and-done proposition. In order to stay connected, we need to stay communicating.

This is similar to how we encourage married couples. I've been married to my lovely wife, Jill, for more than thirty years. During that time, I've traveled relentlessly for work, and yet we've maintained the discipline of a weekly date night. In all of our years of marriage and all those business trips, I haven't missed more than a handful of those date nights.

When you're connected through a vision, in this case our vision of our lives together, it's not something you can neglect. We have to keep working on it to keep the vision alive. In my case, there were times when I couldn't get a flight out, so I rented a car and drove home. We have a shared vision of marriage, though, and so we work hard at it.

FRAMING FOR SUCCESS

Early on, our vision for a successful marriage was simple: we were committed to never getting a divorce.

Over time, though, we came to realize that such a small vision was doomed to failure. It wasn't compelling enough. Simply committing to *not* splitting, while a noble pursuit, didn't feel like enough of a commitment. It stemmed from a negative mindset, and frankly, simply existing as a married couple wasn't a great goal, in and of itself. That was not a compelling vision.

We adjusted. We both said, "Screw this concept of simply

avoiding divorce. That's not big enough for us." So what we chose to do instead was strive not just for a marriage that would last but also one that would achieve excellence. Our vision wasn't just to *be* married but to also have a great and wonderful marriage.

Small visions, no matter how well intentioned, are never going to carry the day. They are never going to be the biggest vision in the room.

And as we will see in the next chapter, the biggest vision in the room always wins.

CHAPTER FIVE

The Biggest Vision in the Room Always Wins

Big visions can come in small packages, but ultimately, the successful ones—the visions that move entire companies, societies, and even nations—are always the biggest ones in any room they occupy. Visions need to be big enough to move people to action, and to encompass the individual visions of all the people in the organization. One of my favorite examples of this comes from the life of Mother Teresa.

She is revered for her work tending to the poor, mostly in India, and for founding the Missionaries of Charity. I like to say that she had a really small, big vision. Her vision was not to eliminate all poverty; it was instead to simply serve the poorest of the poor. Having this core vision guided her to serve more than 120 countries for five decades and led the Roman Catholic Church to proclaim her a saint. Her vision was small in its focus on the extremely poor, but it came to be large enough to spread throughout the world.

THE MORAL COMPASS

Successful leaders are often guided by a distinct moral compass that guides them to big visions, whether it's Mother Teresa and her religious order or the CEO struggling to align his or her company with their own moral code. Not everyone is born with the desire to travel across the world and minister to the poor, but it's an intrinsic desire of human beings to want to improve the world within their sphere, to have an impact on people.

Technology leaders are not immune to this idea either. Cutting-edge companies and their leadership are always worried about bringing "disruptive" change to their industries, change that truly alters the landscape for whatever segment of the economy they occupy.

Tesla is a great example of this. Former CEO Elon Musk wasn't really interested in a car company. What he was truly excited about and interested in changing was energy—how we make it, what we do with it once we have it, its possibilities. He was driven by a vision for a cleaner ecosystem, which in turn would improve the world.

IT'S OK TO BE A LITTLE CRAZY

One of the hallmarks of any big vision is that it is also a little outlandish. We have always loved visionaries who tilt at windmills. There is something compelling about leaders who undertake outlandish quests. Consider Elon Musk again. His vision is absolutely outlandish: space travel, colonizing other planets, cheap renewable energy. As each year passes and Musk turns ever larger pieces of this vision into reality, the outlandish vision becomes less so.

To be truly big, the biggest vision in the room needs to be a little crazy too.

The vision should be so outlandish that it causes people to pause. Audacity is attractive. A big vision that's also a little bit crazy will be a siren song to the kinds of people who are looking to connect to something larger than themselves.

JFK AND THE FIRST OUTLANDISH VISION

A great example of an outlandish vision that actually

came to fruition is President John F. Kennedy's assertion during a Houston speech in September 1962 that we'd put astronauts on the moon before the end of the decade. It seemed ludicrous at the time. America had only recently launched its first manned Mercury missions and were beaten by the Soviet Union at every step at that point in the space race.

Just over a year later, JFK was assassinated, and yet his vision was large enough, and enough people had connected to it, that it persisted despite the loss of its main proponent. Not only that, but when Neil Armstrong stepped foot on the moon in July 1969, the project was six months ahead of schedule.

It's a great example of the power of an outlandish vision, one so powerful that even death cannot stop it from completion.

We choose to go to the moon! We choose to go to the moon this decade, and do the other things, not because they are easy, but because they are hard; because that goal will serve to organize and measure the best of our energies and skills, because that challenge is one that we are willing to accept, one we are unwilling to postpone, and one we intend to win, and the others, too.

—PRESIDENT JOHN F. KENNEDY, SEPTEMBER 12, 1962

The goal is the important part of this whole enterprise. It becomes the invisible hand that makes things happen.

THE BIG VISION IS ROCKET FUEL

Another way to think of needing a big vision is to think of it as propulsive. A powerful and compelling vision, communicated often and connected to leaders and the led, is like rocket fuel for achieving massive results. One ingredient in formulating this propellant is emotion.

When it comes to having the biggest vision in the room, logic will get you only so far. Emotion is the thing that makes people act. If your big vision fails to evoke emotion in your people, it won't be as effective as planned.

THE ART OF SAYING NO

Former British prime minister Tony Blair once said that the art of leadership is saying no. A predecessor of his, Margaret Thatcher, was famous for pointing out the unimportance of being liked. In practice, though, leaders often avoid saying no because they're more concerned with being liked.

In some professions, this concern has real implications on longevity. For example, the federal government's fiscal year begins on October 1. By the end of September, politicians are scrambling to protect any program they think their constituents want, no matter its worth or merit. A politician's career depends on being liked (since *liked* equals *votes*), and their inability to say no becomes destructive and expensive to the country over time.

Highly successful people do less. It's not that they aren't working hard, but they focus their energies on fewer things. Successful people know when to say no. For most leaders, this is counterintuitive, but it's the essence of great leadership.

SAYING NO TO PROTECT THE VISION

The most important reason to say no is to protect your vision. It is too easy to get sidetracked from the vision if you let yourself be moved this way or that. Mother Teresa was called to minister to the poorest of the poor. What would have happened if she had entertained other opportunities that were related to but not in concert with alleviating the misery of the poor? Going out of her chosen lane would have compromised the larger vision.

For those truly committed to their vision, it does not matter how enticing these ancillary offers might be. If it is not part of your vision, you have to say no. This can be a difficult concept to grasp for highly successful, type A personalities. No is almost impossible for these folks to say. But protecting the vision is the priority of any leader, and the best way to achieve that is to decline to engage in anything that moves you off target from that vision.

Probably the starkest example of saying no to protect the vision comes to us from the Ford Motor Company. Ford is emblematic of American automotive prowess. Its founder, Henry Ford, literally invented the production line, which, though staffed mostly by robots these days, remains the main mechanism for car assembly in the world.

Ford, though, just announced they're saying no to the passenger car, which has been the bread and butter of its success for more than one hundred years. The business model has changed, and Ford knows it. To protect its vision as an auto manufacturing power, Ford is going to make the Mustang, light trucks, pickup trucks, and SUVs. As a company, Ford has decided to say no to what was once the foundation of the company in order to survive the next one hundred years.

START WITH THE WHY

Simon Sinek famously admonishes people to "start with the why." If saying no protects the vision, starting with why is its anchor. Be frank with yourself when you talk about this. If money is the sole reason you're pursuing your vision, do not shy away from that. If that's your only vision, you should have the guts and transparency to come out and say it.

The problem, of course, is that such a shallow vision—understanding that money is neither good nor bad, just what you do with it—probably won't resonate with enough people to attract them to your vision.

Ideally, your *why* needs to connect your vision to a larger goal.

Take a look at Bombas socks. Like any company, they want to make money. Their vision, though, is larger than simply making a profit by selling socks. Their why includes trying to improve the lives of their fellow humans, so the business model calls for them to donate a pair of socks to the disadvantaged and homeless for every pair they sell.

Mixing altruism and business can work, but only when it is done from true passion, not as a one-time, throw-away thing. It's evident when the passion is not there. For example, does anyone believe that Dallas Mavericks owner Mark Cuban was passionate about giving $10 million to a women's group?

Cuban paid the money in response to an investigation in fall 2018 that found widespread sexual harassment and discrimination within the Mavericks' front office, as first reported in *Sports Illustrated*. The payment was really an attempt to throw money at a problem, not to honestly address the failings in the corporate culture he was a part of.

FAT GUY IN A LITTLE COAT

In the movie *Tommy Boy*, comedian Chris Farley portrays a hapless auto parts salesman desperate to continue the legacy of his recently deceased father, who built the company. In his quest to save the company, Farley, who is oversized in all senses of the word, joins up with a skinny twig of a man, his father's right-hand man played by David Spade.

In one memorable scene, Farley's character is trying to cheer up his dour partner by donning the smaller man's sport coat and soulfully singing, "Faaat guy in a liiiittle coat," over and over, until he inevitably tears the coat down the middle.

A leader with a small vision is like someone trying to put their extra-small coat on an extra-large person. Every person in an organization brings to the operation a vision of themselves. The leader's vision needs to be not only the biggest in the room but also big enough to contain the vision of everyone under them. If the leader's vision is too small to encompass everyone else's...fat guy in a little coat.

EMPOWERING PEOPLE TO ACHIEVE THE VISION

Thus far, most of our discussion has centered on setting the stage for your vision, from creation, communication, and connection to ensuring that your vision is the biggest in any room. In the next chapter, we'll work on putting the vision into practice through empowerment.

"It doesn't make sense to hire smart people and tell them what to do," Steve Jobs famously said. "We hire smart people so they can tell us what to do."

CHAPTER SIX

Empowerment

In 1996, Bill Parcells was coming off a Super Bowl year, having guided the previously moribund New England Patriots, whom he'd inherited in 1993 after the team won only two games the year before.

Almost immediately, Parcells turned the team into winners. The team earned a trip to Super Bowl XXXI after the 1996 season, which resulted in a loss to the Green Bay Packers. After the season, Parcells abruptly resigned, uttering this famous line:

"They want you to cook the dinner. At least they ought to let you shop for some of the groceries. Okay?"

He referred to the decision by team owner Robert Kraft to limit Parcells's ability to choose the players the team drafted. Parcells had a way with the quip, but his ire exposed a component that the Patriots lacked, at least in Parcells's case: empowerment.

Parcells did not feel empowered by his leadership, and his connection to Kraft through their until-then shared vision broke down.

A NEW MODEL

Leadership used to be about command and control. That model, though, is broken. Today's best leaders are collaborative. Our best leaders are building a collaborative environment and leading through that.

In my generation, the baby boomers, command and control was wielded by the smartest person in the room. This was the guy with all the answers, and everything went through him. Leaders get results through the work of others, so anything that limits the number of people in a position to be successful also limits the size of the success.

Steve Jobs—who said he didn't hire smart people to tell them what to do, but he hired smart people so they could tell *him* what to do—understood that a company's real wealth lies not with the person in charge but with the people they're leading.

EMPOWERING BEGINS WITH CARING

More than two decades ago, television program *60 Minutes* ran a profile of billionaire businessman Jim Goodnight, founder and CEO of SAS Institute, a global technology firm in Cary, North Carolina.

The story focused on the perks of working at SAS headquarters. The lunchroom had linen tablecloths and fine china on the tables. SAS offered concierge services to its employees and built a private school and a golf community that allowed workers to purchase home sites at reduced prices.

The reporter asked Jim, "Why would you do all this?"

"Because, at five o'clock, 95 percent of my company's assets leave the building," he said. "It's my job to make sure they come back."

That was 1995. Today, the company remains one of the absolute leaders in technology information and one of the best places to work in the country.

THE FIVE STEPS FOR THE CARE AND FEEDING OF TALENT

For my money, there is nothing as important in empowerment as how one finds, nurtures, and rewards the people you bring into an organization. These people bring the talent and drive to the task of making your vision a reality. *Empowerment* is a great word that gets thrown around in a lot of contexts, but for our purposes, empowerment, as I envision it, is made up of five components: hiring, investing, releasing, rewarding the talent, and letting the talent reward you.

HIRE TALENT

As Jobs knew, the first task is to hire the talent that's going to get the results your company needs. From there, the next big task is to invest in that talent and set your people up for success.

I learned this firsthand while building a real estate organization. My boss, Mike McCarthy, hired me to run a region that was bringing in about $4 billion in business annually. Within three years, I'd boosted that to $13 billion.

Mike had seen something in me and charged me with developing his offices in that region. In addition to the business growth, we also doubled the size of the staff from four thousand to eighty-two hundred and made a 300 percent increase in owner profits.

Initially, I rebuffed his attempts to hire me. It wasn't a job I had applied for. He'd heard of me through a mutual acquaintance. I turned Mike down three times, but eventually, I came to connect with him through our shared vision and accepted his offer.

INVEST IN THE TALENT

It was a trial by fire. In the first sixty-two days, I visited fifty offices in five states on a listening tour of the company. Every day, we'd debrief about what I had learned and from whom. I appreciated Mike's commitment to the process because it assured him that I was the right person for the job while also letting me know that I was ready for it too.

During this period, I wasn't producing anything yet. This process was pure investment for Mike with no guarantee it would be worth it. It paid off for him in the end, but the risk was real.

RELEASE THE TALENT

This is the third phase of empowerment and the most important. After you've hired the talent and then invested in it, it's time to release it into the world. This was an important lesson from the boss. Once he knew I was prepared, he allowed me to own it.

My boss empowered me to exercise ownership in the duties he had entrusted to me. This was an important point because it avoided the Parcells situation, where a team member has been hired for their skill and acumen, then not allowed to use it.

REWARD THE TALENT

Rewarding your people is not simply about how you pay them. Financial opportunity is an important component, but there are other important ways to reward the people working for you.

Bringing additional resources to bear on the work at hand is one reward. If you can make the work component of your employees' job easier, more efficient, and more productive, that is reward in itself. Training opportunities are also a great reward. Everyone appreciates a chance to be better at their profession.

Sometimes it pays to ask yourself what reward means the most to your people. I once wanted to reward the best executive assistant I had ever had. My plan was to simply bump her salary, but for some reason, it occurred to me to try something new with her.

"April, you're doing such a great job, I'd like to reward you," I said. "I've got two options. One, you can take a 10 percent raise, effective immediately, or two, you can have every other Friday off."

To my surprise, April chose the time off. Her productivity soared on the four days she worked. She was thrilled, and it cost me nothing to do it for her. The thing I realized is that if I had not stopped to ask her what she wanted, I might have done something that cost me money but meant very little to her. Instead, she was even more committed to me as the guy who gave her every other Friday off.

LET THE TALENT REWARD YOU

This is the flip side of the previous component. It should be the natural result of all the work and investment you undertook to get to this point. As we will discuss in a later chapter, a leader gets their results through other people. All the work the leader puts into their vision—nurturing it, communicating it, protecting it—ultimately results in a payoff when the talent you've brought on to accomplish the vision actually does.

For example, it took my boss, Mike, almost twenty years to get to a point where his business had four thousand employees and $4 billion in sales. He'd done amazing work building his company. He also had the vision to know that he needed other people to carry out his vision, and in me, he saw an important piece. Once he hired me, I helped drive growth and raised those totals to eight thousand employees and $13 billion in sales. I reaped many benefits from this performance, but you have to know Mike did too. His commitment to seeing through these first four steps with me resulted in a boost to his bottom line.

WHAT TO DO WHEN IT GOES WRONG

Empowerment is a two-way street. Leadership needs to empower the led to accomplish their shared vision, but there is an onus on the led to take that empowerment and run. Connection with the leader through the vision is what gives the impetus to make this run. The leader has invested in their people, trained them, and provided the resources and autonomy to operate.

We will talk more about accountability in the next chapter, but part of empowerment is inspecting the work of the people you've entrusted to get it done. As mentioned earlier, the Marines have a saying: inspect, don't expect. When you empower people to do a job, your purpose then becomes to ensure that that job is in fact being completed.

A good leader has to ensure that they're inspecting the people they've empowered, then acting quickly when it becomes clear that the vision is not being accomplished. Inspect, don't expect.

THE SEAGULL LEADER

Empowerment can lead to detachment. The worst thing you can do is to become a seagull leader.

This is the type of leader who floats around up in the sky all day, swooping in at the last moment to shit on people. The result is a lack of ongoing consistency. Despite the fact that the leader's action is justified, possibly, enough squawking and defecating, and people are going to stop listening.

The key here is the difference between leadership and management. They are not the same thing. Course correction, fixing things when they break down, is best accomplished on an ongoing basis, not in intermittent bursts of displeasure and anger.

NO PRESSURE, NO DIAMONDS

Empowerment is a powerful tool but only in the hands of people with the discipline and grit to complete missions assigned to them. In the next chapter, we'll discuss accountability, which is the mechanism that makes the rest of this work.

Discipline is often defined as doing what one is supposed to do regardless of whether anyone is watching. Accountability is the way you make sure someone is actually watching. Being held accountable certainly results in pressure, but as the old saying goes, no pressure, no diamonds.

CHAPTER SEVEN

Accountability

A direct report of mine, Mo Anderson, who eventually became the first female CEO of Keller Williams International, was affectionately known as the "Velvet Hammer." She was pleasant and professional but also a consummate professional unafraid to hold those above and below her in the hierarchy accountable.

While she worked with me, doctors discovered a lemon-sized tumor on my neck. Surgery was scheduled, and the week before, Mo and I had our weekly accountability call. It did not begin the way most people might think.

"I know you have that surgery next week," she said. "You might want to double up on your activities this week because you're likely going to be out of commission for the week after."

Whenever I tell this story, I'm often greeted with disbelief. Most seem to expect either shock that she'd suggest I spend my time worrying in the face of a potentially life-altering diagnosis or that I'd simply agree to her suggestion and react accordingly.

By that time, though, Mo and I had had a working relationship for more than two years. I had paid attention, and I told her so.

"Yes, ma'am," I said. "Mo, you've already taught me to plan ahead for things like this, and I'm on it."

Part of her accountability plan was that absences from the office were never an excuse for not doing the work. We planned ahead, and we anticipated contingencies. I'm sure that if I had been hit by a bus, the response would have been, "We should have had a Jim-gets-hit-by-a-bus plan to ensure we can still function."

ACCOUNTABILITY AS AN ACT OF COMPASSION

The opposite of love is not hate. The opposite of love is apathy, the absence of caring. When a leader considers how to hold their people accountable, they need to remind themselves that what they are really doing is an act of love.

Mo Anderson could have spent her time on pursuits other

than holding me accountable. In the overall scheme of things, the company I ran was a small part of her revenue. Her commitment to my execution and to holding me to a high standard was for my benefit, not hers. I had achieved a 300 percent increase in owner profit in my business, but that was not going to change her bottom line or financial picture. She was concerned instead with growing me as a leader, pouring knowledge into me, and helping me improve.

It's a powerful lesson for a leader. Accountability is not about simply tracking achievement and execution. Keeping an eye on your people is fundamentally an act of kindness toward them and a demonstration of your care and concern for them.

THE KEYS TO ACCOUNTABILITY

In an organization that properly holds its people accountable, the leader fosters that atmosphere through four key attributes: culture, commitment, standards, and expectations.

CULTURE

The other three attributes of accountability stem from this first idea surrounding the ethos of your organization. What does it stand for? What is it like to work there, and what types of people do you seek?

Culture can be hard to define, but you know when you see one that's strong and a culture that lacks substance. Harken back to the idea of a vision that isn't lived out as being mere words on a wall. Culture is a lot like that.

COMMITMENT

This is a hard one to train, but it is imperative that every member feels committed to the organization, from the top to the bottom, in both directions, and everywhere in between.

STANDARDS

Culture drives the standards to which you hold your people. The best leaders understand as part of their vision that the organization either has high standards or has none at all. Your culture sets the standards, but the standards are the way you ensure the culture is strong.

There are two subsets of people: those who follow the rules and those who think rules are made to be broken. This second group, though, will adhere to the standards you set. They may not be interested in following arbitrary rules, but they are willing to go the extra mile to hit a standard. These folks have the ability to work within a rule structure, but they are unable to fail at hitting the standard.

EXPECTATIONS

Living up to the standards of the organization is one thing, but to give them power, you pair those standards with clear expectations. Incorporating clear expectations into the standards you've set provides the wind behind your organization's sails.

PUTTING IT ALL TOGETHER

When accountability lacks, problems and issues arise constantly, forcing leaders to play a constant game of Whac-A-Mole, smacking down problem after problem. This is inefficient, at best.

The crisis mindset occurs when these pieces of the puzzle are absent. Leaders have to build a culture that people can commit themselves to. That culture has to be reinforced by high standards, and there have to be clear expectations for how members achieve those standards and contribute to the culture. Accountability is the mechanism that allows leaders to know whether all four traits are present or which ones are absent.

CAREFRONTATION

Inevitably, holding people accountable leads to the occasional difficult discussion. Course correcting an errant team member can be a daunting prospect, especially if the member's issues have been manifold and repeated enough that you have arrived at the "come to Jesus" meeting, the last-ditch effort to square away and retain your troublesome employee.

Having that conversation is an example of true caring. It is both caring *and* confrontation, a concept I like to call *carefrontation*. Currently, fewer leaders are willing to have that confrontation than ever before. It is a growing problem.

Carefrontation is the embodiment of that earlier idea that apathy is the opposite of love, not hate. If I really care about a person in my organization, I need the intestinal fortitude to confront them when their performance demands it. This is a concept that has application beyond the world of business.

At the end of the day, my goal is to ensure these people take ownership in their own growth. I cannot care more about your business than you do. Mo Anderson had that combination that makes carefrontation work so well: she truly cared for her people, and she had the intestinal fortitude to confront them when needed. She was concerned about my health and the tumor in my neck, but she also had a responsibility as my leader to ensure my business performed well, regardless of surrounding circumstances.

DON'T HAVE TO LIKE IT; JUST HAVE TO DO IT

There is an old saying that applies well to the idea of holding your people accountable:

"You don't have to like it; you just have to do it."

As a leader, you do not have to relish the idea of holding your people accountable, but you sure as heck need to do it. In the end, holding your people accountable is what builds your relationship. The mistake leaders often make is to attempt to establish a relationship with their people first and then hope the results follow.

This is backward and guarantees the results will most likely never happen. Establishing the relationship first, then hoping they achieve results, guarantees that you will be forced to shed people you like but who failed to get the results you need. Using accountability and carefrontation to get results first will lead to genuine relationships.

CONSISTENCY IS KEY

Accountability is all about consistency—offering consistent weekly feedback, week in and week out. The Mo Anderson conversation related earlier in the chapter was one of a couple of hundred we had in three years. The reality of most of those calls was that Mo used them to reinforce the things I was doing right. She held me accountable, which included ensuring that I continued to do things that worked.

It can be a grind. The more direct reports a leader has, the more time they'll need to spend holding the accountability line with their people. Part of success is grinding it out. Another lesson from Mo was that consistent accountability was important enough to her that she remained committed to it even as her star rose in the corporate world. Even as demands on her time skyrocketed, every Monday morning at 8:30 we were on the phone or meeting in person. It was a powerful lesson.

When I was in the middle of growing the $4 billion real estate business into a $13 billion business, I put Mo's lessons to good use. Despite the number of people working for me, I made sure that I talked to every one of my operators at least twice a month. The employees I talked to had to feel like they toiled in anonymity, but they got amazing results, and the act of monitoring their performance and giving consistent feedback let them know that they were in fact doing the job well.

THE SANDWICH METHOD

As I've said, consistency is the key, and I prefer to give my people tremendous amounts of feedback on a regular basis. To make this effort more useful, I often rely on a rubric that allows me to praise good work while effectively pointing to areas that could use improvement in such a way as to leave the recipient both educated and energized rather than demoralized.

When I offer feedback as part of the accountability process, I often envision my criticism as a sandwich. Each layer of the sandwich represents a different aspect of the accountability conversation with an employee, which usually begins and ends on a positive note (depending on the difficulty of the necessary discussion).

The top layer of bread in the sandwich is positive feedback. I like to spend the first part of our sessions highlighting areas where my employee excels. This sets the groundwork for a productive session, as opposed to punitive, and puts them in the right frame of mind for the next part.

The meat in the middle represents constructive criticism. This is your opportunity to point out areas for improvement. No matter how close to perfection any of us comes, there are always things we could do better. The point is not to dwell on what the employee is doing incorrectly, but it is important to cover things that aren't as good as they could be.

The bottom layer of bread represents additional positive feedback. As the old saying goes among comedians, always leave on a high note. The sandwich method is a journey, albeit brief, and ending on a high note is important because those good feelings are going to lead to energy, and that energy is what will help your employee do their best work.

THE PROCESS

The accountability processes I set up for my people break down into three categories: set expectations, track and monitor results, and give consistent feedback.

SET EXPECTATIONS

We have discussed these earlier, but they bear repeating. Setting expectations up front makes it clear exactly what your people need to achieve. They know the results you demand and the targets they need to hit. In addition, leaders will set the expectations the employees should have of the leaders themselves. In my own practice, I set expectations for what they can expect from me, right down to the level of honesty I offer in my accountability sessions.

TRACK AND MONITOR RESULTS

Tracking and monitoring your team's results has many benefits, but chief among them is clarity as to whether you've done a good job communicating and connecting through the vision. There is no doubt about the efficacy of your efforts when the results are clear and easily evaluated.

A great example of tracking and monitoring results is the venerable and low-tech Christmas club account many of us had as kids. Saving money for Christmas is a yearlong struggle, which Christmas club accounts cleverly solved. Every week in the months before Christmas, holders of this kind of account would deposit money that the bank made available for withdrawal only during the holiday season, the idea being to save money for presents.

The success of the Christmas club was a quick and easy way to track and monitor the results of your attempt to save money in time to buy presents. The results are instantly available and easy to interpret, key factors in any assessment process. It is fair to note that tracking and monitoring is a big part of the "grind" aspect of accountability but an important piece too.

GIVE CONSISTENT FEEDBACK

This is another aspect of accountability that bears repeating. Much like ceaseless communication of the vision as an important job for the leader, feedback needs to be frequent and consistent. Mo Anderson always carved out time for me. I ensured I met often with all my leaders no matter how busy I might otherwise have been. None of this works without clear, consistent feedback.

GETTING RESULTS THROUGH OTHER PEOPLE

Next we'll discuss an uncomfortable truth: none of us is LeBron James. No matter the field of endeavor, none of us can carry the load ourselves. The best leaders understand this. We get results through other people.

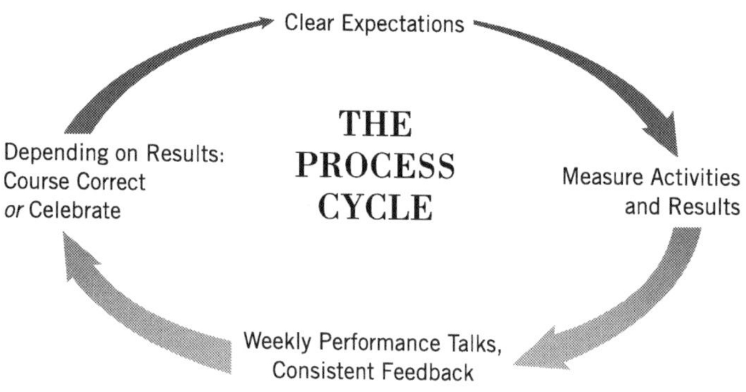

CHAPTER EIGHT

You're Not LeBron James

I've spent more than thirty-five years in real estate. My career almost ended after just six months.

I was twenty-two and just out of college and apprenticing in a real estate office run by a man named Sam Chalfont. I was building my business but not making any real money. To supplement my income, I worked a second job as a security guard on the overnight shift for another forty hours a week. After six months, I was exhausted and had little to show for it, other than early glimmers of evidence suggesting I was going to be good at selling real estate.

I approached Sam and told him I had to quit.

"I just can't do this anymore," I said. "I appreciate everything you've done for me, but I've got to stop."

"Quit that second job," he said. "You're going to be good at this, I can tell. Don't give up."

Then he went to his desk drawer, took out his checkbook, and wrote me a check for $10,000. That's a lot of money even today, but in the early 1980s? Staggering.

He said, "I believe in you. Take this ten thousand bucks; it's yours. If you need more, let me know."

I never cashed that check. I was able to persevere without his money, but the courage his belief gave me was worth more than any money. This profound act affected me deeply, and it is part of the reason I coach people today.

RESULTS THROUGH PEOPLE

What Sam understood was the value of cultivating your best employees, and in the long run, the results that he foresaw me generating more than offset the investment of $10,000 in my talent and potential.

Sam's bet paid off. I took his advice and ended up winning Rookie of the Year for the office. He didn't write that check without knowing exactly what he was investing in.

Sam was a great leader. He spent lots of time monitoring and tracking my work, holding me accountable, and he gave me practical tools on a consistent basis. He knew I had the potential to grow into a valuable member of his team, and he was willing to put money behind this belief. He was more interested in raising a great team around himself rather than basking in a dimmer glow focused on himself alone.

Professional sports are a great proving ground for this theory.

The better team will always win out over the team with the single best player. The best player in the universe does not win championships. The best team—the best assemblage of talent—does.

A great leader knows that any results they generate come through the people on their team. Basketball powerhouse LeBron James is the most supremely talented basketball player on the planet, but the knock on him has been that he does little to improve the players around him. In LeBron's case, this does not preclude championships. There has been only one LeBron, though.

You are not LeBron.

At best, you are Michael Jordan. True, he brought once-in-a-hundred-years talent to the game, but he *also* made it a point of improving the players who joined him on the court. His Chicago Bulls teams were some of the best in the history of the game, mainly because they were teams first and foremost.

Even Michael Jordan knew he needed to get results through other people. You need to learn that lesson too.

HELPING YOUR TEAM SUCCEED WITHOUT YOU

Leaders often have difficulty admitting that they need other people to get the results they want. Most are high achievers who, left to their own devices, could get great results. To maximize results, though, leaders need teams of people just like them. The goal is to set the team up for success in such a way that they can succeed without you.

In my experience, there are four steps a leader can take to ensure that they're building a team that does not need them:

- Empower
- Equip
- Encourage
- Enable

EMPOWER

We've already spent an entire chapter discussing the importance of empowerment, and it remains relevant as one of the core means to get results through people. I also like to think of empowerment as your "constitutional right" to get a job done.

EQUIP

Equipping your teams can come in many forms. Perhaps it's training or the actual tools to accomplish whatever job you've given them or simply having an office space ready for new employees on their first day.

Equipping can also take the form of frequent and consistent feedback, the kind that gives you the feedback and skills necessary for success.

ENCOURAGE

Very few people are 100 percent successful at all times. As leaders, we need to know who needs that little boost of confidence and care enough about them and the organization to ensure we offer encouragement.

ENABLE

When you put it all together, you enable your team to

carry out the vision and achieve better results than you could ever have predicted. In a larger sense, you give your team permission to be great, and it is this enabling that leads to growth and results. The cumulative efforts of Sam Chalfont were what enabled me to perform for him, and I was one of many people through whom he got his results.

MONEY ISN'T THE ONLY MEASURE

Everyone has a moment of crisis, an instance when we no longer believe in ourselves. The day I went to Sam and told him I needed to quit was one such day for me. It is human nature. I survived my moment of crisis, but it was not because of the money he offered me. The money was a symbol of his faith in me and my future. I didn't need it, though. What I needed more was his encouragement.

Money isn't the only measure of how we treat the people we lead. We all have moments of doubt, and in that time of crisis, that is when leaders are required to come alongside their people. Having Sam believe in me was the moment that has made all the difference to me. It was the epitome of the idea of getting results through people.

I continue to get results today based on the example Sam showed me back in the day.

Sam got results through people. He was a quiet leader. He wasn't going to scream and yell and carry on. He was almost nondescript, which stood out in the 1980s, an era of relentless self-promotion. He moved behind the scenes, and he got results.

THE LEADER SHOULD ONLY BE OUT FRONT AFTER A MISTAKE

Leadership is not about ego. At least, it shouldn't be. Leaders take ownership of the results their organizations deliver, but a good leader is only out front if there's been a mistake. A certain amount of self-promotion can add value, but great leaders care about their people. They want to get results through them, but they also want to see their people benefit overall.

It can either be about your people or about you but never both.

An organization is only going to go as far as your people do. The baby boomer generation was taught that leadership meant a hard-charging, big personality with all the answers. This was the ideal leadership style. In recent years, there has been a paradigm shift. Leaders who embrace it will get amazing results if, and only if, they get those results through other people.

COMMIT TO THE GRIND

There is a grind to doing all that work behind the scenes. To push the sports analogy some more, though, ask yourself this: Where are championships won? Exactly: behind the scenes, on practice fields, or in weight rooms.

A leader has to have a commitment to the grind. Part of that grind is to care for the people who work for you, who are connected to you through the vision you created, who are communicated with in the first place.

Leaders need to care enough about their people to be willing to monitor and track the results they deliver, give them consistent feedback, and empower, equip, encourage, and enable them. If you accomplish all of those things, it is inevitable: you will get results through your people.

CHOSEN

One of my favorite verses from the Bible, John 15:16, talks about how we often do not have a say in the things we are chosen to do. As I have spent time thinking about getting results through people, this verse has come to mind frequently. It speaks to this idea of a leader being asked to bear fruit.

In this case, results are the fruit, and your legacy will be the people whom you led to get those results.

You did not choose me, but I chose you and anointed you so that you might go and bear fruit—fruit that will last—and so that whatever you ask in my name, the Father will give you.

—JOHN 15:16

This verse provides five clear insights on leadership:

1. As a leader, you were chosen
2. You've been given the talent, tools, and skills to lead
3. You are expected to get results
4. Your people and your results are your legacy
5. You are expected to ask for help

Conclusion

This book is a distillation of almost four decades of experience leading, teaching, and mentoring leaders. I have dedicated my life to the study of leadership, and in my judgment, there is no single piece of the puzzle more central to the success of any organization than its guiding vision.

It is not enough to simply have read this or any other book on the subject without putting the knowledge to use. Education without implementation is just entertainment. There is a time for study and a time for putting it to use, and for you, that time is now. I always tell my people, "Work works." I realize that is a heuristic, a thing that defines itself, but it is still true.

Successful leadership begins with a vision, communicating that vision to the troops, and then connecting with them through the shared vision. The other pieces are just as important. Leaders need to consistently hold their people accountable, monitor and track results, and set clear expectations.

The most important lesson of this book is to realize that it is only the beginning. The biggest, most compelling, well-communicated, and successful vision is not a lottery ticket. Putting the principles in here to use is going to take lots of hard work and dedication. The lottery mindset is not a recipe for success, but it is emblematic of the modern approach to success. Buy enough ten-dollar lottery tickets, and eventually, you will win enough money to retire, right?

No.

As any financial planner can tell you, the way to retire with money is to have the discipline to do smart things with your money over the years, such as saving $100 a month of income for forty-five years. It's a simple idea, but it takes dedication, commitment, and discipline, just like having, holding, and protecting a vision for the company or organization you are growing. Creating a great vision and throwing it up on a wall is not enough to achieve your goals, either personal or organizational. Leaders need to do the work to ensure that their vision means something to the people who work with them.

Ultimately, any results you achieve as an organization will be through *those* people. Your personal greatness is almost irrelevant. The important thing is the greatness of the people around you, the team you create, and the vision that guides them all. Individual greatness for a leader is not only not required, but in some cases, it may also be a detriment. A leader such as Elon Musk is almost too big a deal for his own company. Hailed as a once-in-a-generation leader, it is real easy for Musk to read his own press and come to believe it. Worse, public perception ties Tesla's prospects so closely to Musk's personal situation that the number one concern is not with the company products and development, but whether Musk will remain with the company.

It is difficult at best to engage your people in the work if the driving force in pursuit of achieving the organization's vision is the leader's own personal greatness. We are not, after all, LeBron. We cannot achieve our goals alone. However, when you've done enough work on communicating a big vision and connecting through it to your employees, if you've held them and yourself accountable to living out and pursuing that vision, success is assured.

WHAT YOU SHOULD DO NEXT

I hope that while reading this book it's become clear to you that everything begins and ends with the leader, and their willingness and diligence to do the work in creating, communicating, and carrying out a vision. The work has to begin with *you*. Ask yourself a few questions:

- Do I have a clear vision for the organization?
- Do I really believe in the vision? Do I "own" it?
- Do I understand how executing this vision will change our part of the world?
- Have I done my best to ensure everyone in the organization has heard it many times?
- Do they know the vision?
- Can they tell me the vision?
- Can they share how their lives will be better when the vision is accomplished?
- Are my people buying into the vision? Are we connected?
- Have I done my best to hold people accountable?
- Do I really care about my people?
- Do I care enough to make them uncomfortable with feedback?
- Do I see the success of my people as my real "scorecard"?

This insight—that vision and communication are the pillars on which everything else is built in your organization—is key to your evolution as a leader. If the biggest vision in the room always wins, this insight is the biggest vision of them all.

About the Author

JIM FISCHETTI is an ultrasuccessful leader, innovator, and consultant who has spent more than fifty thousand hours coaching and developing leaders throughout corporate America. In addition, he's spoken to more than sixty thousand people and has helped their organizations find scale and success, increasing sales from $4 billion to $13 billion.

A lifelong student of leadership who's spent four decades refining his notions of what makes a great and transformative leader, Jim is committed to helping others understand the importance of vision in their lives, and this commitment extends to his work outside the corporate world, as a mentor to nonprofits and married couples in his church.

Jim lives with his best friend and wife of thirty-three years, Jill, in Raleigh, North Carolina.

To contact Jim, please email JimFischetti@gmail.com, or visit www.coachwithjim.com.

Made in the USA
Monee, IL
25 February 2020

22302883R00081